Environmental F(r)iction
The Illusion of Progress
← →
The Progress of Illusion

Bill F. Ndi

Langaa Research & Publishing CIG
Mankon, Bamenda

Publisher:

Langaa RPCIG
Langaa Research & Publishing Common Initiative Group
P.O. Box 902 Mankon
Bamenda
North West Region
Cameroon
Langaagrp@gmail.com
www.langaa-rpcig.net

Distributed in and outside N. America by
African Books Collective
orders@africanbookscollective.com
www.africanbookscollective.com

ISBN-10: 9956-550-51-5

ISBN-13: 978-9956-550-51-7

Table of Contents

All by Design

Were this world the product of chance, design
Would be an offstage clown left to resign
Its past, present, and future to hazard
And we'd be left with old lady haggard
With just no enticements to lure any
But that with whom to breed dreary phony
In the likes of naysayers with a drift
That can't explain the Continental Drift.
Today, we hear them say of the Greens: "nuts"
For daring to hint Man must not be nuts
To leave the flowers of the universe
In the hands of chance that can't make a verse
About the struggle for the right weapon
That let the monster to grow and move on.

Roundabout Talks

They have just concluded their rounds of talks
And to take stock all thoughts are geared on stocks;
The spindle on which the world makes its move.
Look not for it in *The World on the Move!*
Ah! Those blind historians of yesteryears
Whose thoughts of the Black Death gripped them with
fears
Could not see the rain will one day be gone
As on the right all must stick to the gun
The world is oblivious to Man's efforts
To redeem him from covetous escorts
And their pimps pimping 'tis pleasing to use
Fossil fuel like harlots, and not abuse
While, here at this end our hearts tear of blood
And on our feet we are not left to plod.

The Arrogant and Their Snare

In that world of arrogance criminals
Are hailed for behavior like animals
While the meek who embrace humility
Are greeted with spite and claims "they're silly"
So thinks such world for the creed of the meek
Avoids their snare and doth power above seek
Not such noose with its appeals to senses
By ill-will oblivious to influences
Not benumbed by the master of mischief's
Evil designed snare of flamboyant thieves;
In their stead with molar to molar smile
They refuse to see in this grand plan style
Not man nor creature in flesh and blood
Can envision or distort with a stud.

Why the Cloud Runs

The cloud does not move away from one end
Of the sky with the aim to pretend
All is well wherefrom he has his back turned
And has had memories of such a place burned
To ashes and buried in the dustbin
Of history whose revival produce pin
Pricks in a solace craving heart of gold
Reduced, trampled underfoot, trashed, and sold
For the aggrandizement of lusty ticks
Stuck on the pubic regions to play tricks
The cloud would rather steer clear of to let
All eyes wide open to see the platelet
Blue in daylight with no need for an aid
That would ground the cloud in flight from that raid

Christmas Eve 2015

When Christmas came, hell chose to be angry;
Crossed for 'tis a birthday that brings misery
To his world of darkness averse of light,
The nemesis with whom he has a fight.

I witnessed my yard turned into a pool
And the news showed Boston streets with no wool
Covering the spilled blood of good old Quakers
To bring joys to America as Lakers
This day do to NBA diehard fans
All oblivious to the plight of Afghans.

Cynics a few weeks back mocked at this sign
And styled COP21 human design
To distort the clever Big Bang theory
Claiming accidents as human history.

Wicked Weather

Every now and again the weather claims
Her dues from man's recklessness and with blames
Is greeted and then washed clean with guesses
Far removed from calculated uses
She would rather have had men of her make
To spare her the trouble they take to fake
Their senseless tinkering with nature irks not
Until whole cities are reduced to naught;
This time across three states with fourteen dead
Still, same blind gainsayers flock in a herd
Bleating more need for fossil fuel to burn
With the ash not to be left in an urn:
African, Grecian, Asian, or 'Rican
With climate's claim clearly glued to their plan.

Taking Time and Stock

The second takes the time it takes to push
The minute which takes its turn to ambush
The hour pushing it down the drain the day
Transforms to weeks that come and go than stay
For months never to see light in their pit
Of darkness wherein stately miseries sit
Flashing mounds of fortune to bait gluttons
Whose throats would swallow a cow like pythons'
Projecting to the fore of the tableau
The beauty and the beast without the beau;
Left in a hat for a child to admire
In Antoine de St. Ex…'s world of fire
Devoid but with shinny stars filled for stock
Taking in which world men work not but sock.

Today and Then

Climate change warriors' hearts came to a stop
As the twister hit the highway atop
The buildings it brought down within a blink
In Arlington and Garland who'd not think
Disaster would play its drum on their thin
Skin and turn the streets into a dustbin
Mountain echoing cries of "Had I known"
Sprinting in last with no reason to crown
The chaos he had brought upon the world;
Depleting riverbeds that once swelled
Up to penetrate their fertile life banks
With no means to drain the brains forebears nursed
Against greed and had the art well-rehearsed
Mindless any would ever tell them: "thanks".

Keep the Buoy Afloat

We have cheated nature! We must admit
We give her reason to emit vomit
For she is repulsed by our wrongdoing
And cannot stomach this nonsense rumbling,
An irksome noise our supersonic jet,
Who speeds industry and nature's upset,
Brings with which tragedy we must make do
Or reverse by our kindness to her too
She'd been kind to let the ball in our court
And we played not by the books and must court
Her now to make amends not to nose dive,
The Damocles' sword over us! We strive
To live and make sure nature brings him down
For the buoy to stay afloat and not drown.

Climate Won't Spare the Rod

Make climate change the object of your scorn
And derision you'd see smiles adorn
Him when yours would be mourning at night fall
Mourning the smiles you'd thought would have you
sworn
In the greatest life has ever known born
Of man thinking wise where splendor stands tall
Like a mother with her young firm and keen
Not to spare any rod and spoil her child
Who dreams and thinks of nothing but the bean
He would spew to make his sweet Mother wild
With pitiless flaunting of chastening rod
With goal to do good as would oil from cod
Liver with its nauseous stench that soothes
The frail frame of sick children who trick truths.

Weapon of Deception

The heavens have unleashed their wrath against
Naysayers who seemed bent to be against
Anything that dissuades Man from fiddling
With arrangements made from the beginning
And will be thus till the end that'll ne'er come;
Like Lady Smith's line: "Oh come, Never come"
Sung in praise of rain that is beautiful
For it does not disturb us as we fool
Around in the name of celebration;
In itself, pure cosmic indignation.
Squirting bilious rage from heaven's open
Tap that can't be stopped by the sword or pen,
Weapons leaving Man with the deceptive
Taste for might which with time is destructive.

Man's Pay: Cooling & Boiling

Man would like to see himself as master
Of this universe, though not to better
Or of the universe make a beauty
That would defy the splendor of nature
With her exquisite appeal as pasture
For humans and animals who party
With neither fear nor favor in a bit
To outdo each other stomping their feet
To a tune that invokes an angry feat
In which elephants would beat and drum it
To leave the fields of their battles in ruin
Just to fall back on for the pasture's green
Which green had been butchered through mockery made
Of cooling and boiling with which we're paid.

Scarring the Planet

When would man confess he pulls the trigger
And leave scars on our planet with tiger
Claws he uses not because he's hungry?

When would man admit Nature is angry
At a play that is everything else but fair
In a world where dream merchants do not care?

How does one go about the thought of mare
In which sturdy thugs in the House do chase
Fear from the dupes of thuggery in this case?

What can man do when Nature, in his face,
Spews Her venom by unleashing torrents
Of rains that disregard ocean currents?

The trigger of rage would have its moments;
The need for care shall strike in one minute.

Mindless Willingness

Dinosaurs this world ruled with mindlessness
And nowadays 'tis man with willingness
And claims he's the choicest of creation
Yet, man garbs the same with condescension
Feeding hopes that his wisdom would handle
The darkness brought about by his candle
In the wind; blown out and left with no…. life
Where man's existence should herald his strife.
The mind bent on 'after me the deluge'
Is so twisted that the longing is huge
To have the dream come true to the uncouth
Whose hat displays everything but the truth
And you bet this will free our world from rage
Prompted by man who would be swept offstage.

Rooftop Music

Raindrops on the tin roof in Africa
Play a beautiful music not too far
From this heart that miles and miles faraway
From home still allows her to shine her way
Through the thicket of doubts hiding the rain
Clouds as they recede in show of disdain
For the know-all whose knowledge is nothing
Set besides wisdom infinite musing
In total silence worthy of a church
Yard where there are no trees in sight to perch
But for crosses standing on the remains
Of souls whose lives were marked by quests for gains;
And now reality hits and calls for check,
Too late to be saved by figures on a check.

Farm in the Oven

I tuned to the news and was told the sun
Had just done baking patches of farmlands
And had thrown off farmers with their tear glands
Engaged in fights against the smoking gun
They had refused to take into account
With claims of wisdom which would it obscured
The thinking of those who wish naysayers cured
Of their witlessness that all we count count
When wits have it that not all that's counted
Count and more, not all that counts is counted
So farmers whose livelihood on nature
Depends must learn the art of nursing
And caring for bees that'd without doubt sting
And show them there's a sharp edge of nature.

The Order

Deny and defy nature is angry
It won't take her long to leave you hungry
And in your hunger you'd need her good grace
To fix your meddling attempt to outpace
Her as ye scoff this day; crocodile tears
From your eyes, would come not to wash your fears
For this kind mother holds a chastening rod
She would use when provoked than let you nod
At your own doom and like a coward die
A thousand deaths for you thought hers a lie.
Nature has an order with variables
We needn't take for Sisyphus' pebbles
Pushing our weights too high only to fall
Where we will never, in history, stand tall.

Choices We Make

When the rains came we wept; they said adieu!
And when the sun showed up, we lost our dew
And the tears we shed came from crocodiles
For when we cast lots we didn't dream of piles
Of woes crushing us to make hide and skin
Just when we took hide and seek for a kin;
A choice we had made, and without forethought
That all trees, mountains and rivers are wrought
By the duty conscious and tireless hands
At work to echo sweet music from bands
The hosts play to escort the departed
Who in his life turned his back on nature
Convicted this old dame needs a suture
To fix her broken lining and indeed…

The Rains and Their Love

The rains jilted their love for many years
And for many years the earth embraced fears
For she knew when they came they would wash her
Clean as well as overflow the river
Banks that for these years have starved tenacious
Homo sapiens embracing salacious
Ideas teeming and humming in their heads
With bees who'd turn around and sting the nerds.
Calculation after calculation
Led them to draw a hollow conclusion:
Nature's anger can be contained by man
Who is driven by supply and demand;
An equation that spites hard-to-crack nuts
And proves the wise man can also be nuts.

Of Human Progress

Seventeen million cars sold in twenty
Fifteen sent US dancing for scarcity
Had been slain, downplaying the damage done
To the water in the pot on the throne
Above; fatigued to be overheated
By unconscionable and strong headed
Gainsayers who in science conspiracy
See and send her proofs to be drowned at sea
Wherein the tampering stands between currents
That would their response bring home in torrents
Which torrents leave man's open eyes wide shut
For the licentious is Mr. Big Shot
Shooting and feeding fat on the masses
In our classless culture fraught with creases.

We Call the Rains

This winter the rains came and lulled our sleep
One in which we fell down, down, down the deep
From which we tried to pull ourselves upward
Even though we'd not been the steward
Of repute keeping the earth's health in place
Which we'd taken for granted with a mace
In hand to show the world this might of state
Whence the environs sees a ward of state
In hapless us for when they would unleash
Their wrath for our impertinence, no leash
Would hold them back for this provocation
Calls for anger not her renunciation;
Yet, we give the blame game life with a spin
We are blame free for stretching nature thin.

The Twins

The sun goes to give free rein to the cold
Who in full force comes to outperform gold
In any fairy tale and or legend
Sprawling the walls of our streets without end
And we need not forget the architect
Of such an unfair play they call tech…
Who in complicity with industry
From her uprising left our skies cloudy;
The twins to this day keep pulling a fast
One and would thus, no shadow of doubt cast
Upon the knaves of disciple Thomas
Who hold fast nature plays Father Christmas;
Yet, her true color comes with her vengeance
Though she is in her own right, tolerance.

Gain Makers

With progress they uphold their enterprise
Is one that would win the world the big prize
To solve the crisis they've dragged the climate
Into and would only recall to sit
Up and take action when it is too late
As they are already be in the pit
They'd been digging with claims they control fate;
Some saying they are rain makers and some
Singing own praises as the shining stars
Who give the sun such luster void of scars
And had been rewarded with a handsome
Chunk of the sweat of all the ward of state
Who for their impertinence must the price
Pay for making gain makers shrink their size.

For Brother West

Brother West postured east and gave his speech;
Listeners' ears drank and goad them to screech
For their nerves never had been poked so hard
By any who claims to be an old bard
Witnessing like my brother the season
Of violence in which blackness is treason
And the rape on the environs virtue
The rapists lauded and approved as true
To form in any world where might is right
And the feeble free to put up a fight
They'd never win as their voices are drowned
In the mire of intricate ideas spawned
To make believe body parts are our haps
And in the end there will be no mishaps!

Summer's Fall

Summer came with the look of Brother Fall
And with trees whose lush in him should stand tall;
But their nakedness displayed doth push worms
To the background while none would talk reforms
For their posture is to the right and far
And makes green talk blur the shine of their star
Who would he made the earth the waiting room
Of hell whose ashes do not need a broom
To sweep the burnt out ends of smoky hades
With serpentine trails of a zillion shades
It pukes to scare children who crave a place
In the sun only to realize his face
Has been disfigured by the snaky smoke
That stirs their fight to the left where they'd spoke.

My Friend: The Weatherman

Fix news weatherman, why should I watch you?
The news you bring is neither good nor new
For your stench, man, has fixed everything news
And left you with garbage that your screen spews
And why should I pollute my eyes with such?
Or why must I burden you with this crunch?
None would have to tell me the heat I feel
When I am not bundled up but must peel
My skin to have some air in a poisoned
World that to resell you'll have well-seasoned
As bait for the faint of heart with no sense
But only that with which to take nonsense.
Weatherman before you have the news fixed,
Make no slips, mince no words, have your acts fixed!

Driven by Greed

When the cold penetrates all the layers
I've carefully lain as would bricklayers
To cloister a wall and this with blankets
I won't be that fool they'd take to markets
To have buy their disdain without barter
For when I look up I can't see farther
Than the thick pool of mud pouring down rains
Whose water is only good for the drains.
This cold pricks with her long legged needles
And shakes hunger in my inner noodles
Who would rather be left to sleep in peace
Than have to be bothered about the fleece
They've stolen; driven by nothing but greed
As they ignore our green that all can read.

The Forecast

A fierce snow storm has just been announced
He is on his way ready to pounce
And fear of a lion clawing its preys
Grips the state where congress or house prays
And on their knees in a state of fright
Driving home thoughts their gods are in flight;
And there's no doubt they have spent time
Mockery making: trampling on prime time
The world they can't create and won't protect
For they hold it true that their intellect
Will be exercised to stop disasters
From beating up their makers and masters.
Yet, this beaten and flattened truth, not mine
Makes its mark for, "a stitch in time saves nine".

Advancement

Grandparents and parents looked up in the sky
At night
In the dark
They saw both the moon and stars
That was in the days
And that was life!
Today, they're long gone and won't be back.
A look at the sky this day,
Mark ye!
During the day with the blazing sun up above
Darkness proper greets the eyes
And at best smog caresses them
And stops the sun from bathing us.
Thrown into confusion, I would I were told
Why my days are with darkness filled
And laconic progress thrown at me
To spread gloom and muddle in my vagrant
Mind wandering to and from then and now
For my advancement!

Writing on the Wall

Winter took a trip to the tropics
While tropical draughts unveiled tactics
Used to journey to forbidden lands
Where they melt down ice and scorch farmlands
These sleeping dogs would have lied without
Doubt and troubled no one for coming out
As these days the custom would guarantee
And have people locked in away from free
Outings they take daily and for granted
And would readily have any branded
For daring to suggest men better treat
This globe that's a sacred ground of retreat
For animals, birds, insects, and humans;
Even those taken for lesser humans.

Triumph of the Economies

Smoke blackens the backs of pots and kettles
And men the butt of the skies with squabbles
And hot air that push forth inclemency
And the moon phases to proficiency
In freezing the globe when lone cold's needed
To ward off bombs we don't need exploded
To snap our mouths open with gainsayers'
Even wider as they crave soothsayers
Comfort them theirs is but an accident
Brought about by wind that can't leave a dent
On their Ozymandiac sculpted member
Marooned for none to ever remember
Their condescension for symbiosis
Sacrificed for market economies.

Things in Place

We came and met the rivers and mountains
All in place and their yield; that which sustains
Us seduces our greed and we would we
Changed the course of the rivers 'coz we're free
And think the mountains big mistakes we must
Flatten for if abandoned we would rust
For we think we're made to marry the shine
Of gold whose luster modern men define
As the light with which all must be obsessed
And blindly the weak of heart are possessed
By the demons of this counterfeit light
That lay the foundation of human plight
With humans pitting their wisdom against
The Wisdom Man should not stand up against

Flag of Human Wisdom

We fly our intelligence on a post
To make believe 'tis light on lamppost,
One to take man out of primitiveness
And garb him in civilization's dress
Brushing off consequences with backhand
And they'd come down the line to haunt the land
And would thus come without warning and sign
To leave man with no choice but to resign
His fate to flood and fire, hail, rain and storm
And his astuteness would argue warm
Is far from being the climate his claim
To control only bring his fame to shame
He sees not for his pride and arrogance
Blur his vision and push him to his stance.

Of Chances and Climate

Play all your Russian roulette with seasons
And hope you'd hide yourself in garrisons
Walled with lies and denials that you harm not
That which graciously has been given not
For the good graces and riches men lack
Though with assertions theirs cannot turn back
To look at the lowly and worthless maimed
By their callous greed foreshown, and not shamed
As a monument of dishonor, but
As one housing the climate in a hut
And wishing it will never ever crack
And it will without doubt to stay on track.
Feel free! Take chances! And consequences
Too; they'll not come with packs of surprises.

Tipping the Scale

The vision to make all disposable
Turns trees, grasses, flowers, sun, moon, and stars
To heaps and piles of garbage that would leave scars
To remind of what's indispensable
For a world in dire need of a balance
Which greed would rather knock out of balance
On the scale of production and storage
With equitability out of favor
And exiled to dominions of labor
Hegemons have created for abusage.
These nightmares do raise ghosts in these farmlands
Where cheap labor is provided by hands
Quick to be conned to accept there's a place
In the sun for their likes who don't wear lace.

The Bequest

Eyes stroke by the blue skies delight the hearts
Once drowned in toxic fumes from the backyards
Where man muddies the waters to veil the skies
And throw the climate in the throes of blues
With no nous she'd dance her way in the news.
Dance? She dances to a tune stirred by flies
In a boiling globe that facilitates
Putrefaction, art that does not preserve
And does not want procedure to reserve
The fate carried out with assailed dictates
On the scum of the earth whose woes irk souls
On the way to departure with forethought
Of birthright to bequeath to would be souls
Who'd not settle for gift that can be bought

Climate: Stroke without Lapse

Cold or heat does place hands of discomfort
On the sleep drunk with the shell of cannon
That would bring down the ramparts of the fort
In which man entombs himself far from fun
Having toyed with natural processes
Directing the wind, shaping moon phases
And hoping his toils would spare him the woes
That upset and discard him in the throes
Of rakish nervousness he cries could end
And discharge some endorphins to kill pain
Bought by his trust in nothing but his brain
For he does squirrel away things and trend
His contempt for climate and the mishaps
Brought about by hands which stroke without lapse.

Rover Claims River

Think it wise not to let the river run
And steal the joys of Lord Tennyson's brook
As you applaud your wisdom by the book
For when climate turns its back, on the run
Nowhere shall you have to conceal your shame
And lack of dignity with which you treat
The earth who labors to be our retreat
One in which you've come and would steal its fame
And put your mask of humanness to show
You were with reason gifted though you fail
To see this beauty put to place won't fail
To unveil its splendor where you'd burrow
Warrens to hide loots you'd still leave with her
For she would remain forever river.

Caring and Loving Mother

For the love of life, climate never drops
Her chastening rod to spare unruly man
Who has privilege and creation chart tops;
And does call onto himself reprimand
Through the callousness that in his veins runs
Sending him wild with a hording fever
Gripping and shaking his heart for ever
To be after the material he guns
For to the disgust of Mother Nature;
Caring and loving to stimulate eyes
With the green of leaves and grasses in rice
Fields where the golden grains are a treasure;
A treasure not for the disregarder
Man has made himself trait of character.

Sons that Burns

These treasures we hunt are not the product
Of some accident strewn on the highway
Of this life clearly marked by a short stay
That comes to an end and floods the tear duct
In hope our sorrows and lamentations
Were washed to give birth to suns that won't burn
The loot amassed at every twist and turn
Without forethought we'd have no solutions
To fix that which we receive and abuse
By the hour with chants "we know what's best"
And would warm our planet to stand stress test
Set for men with conducts all would recuse.
Thus treasure hunter needs not poach the game
And make excuses which won't nature tame.

Trapping the Trapper

Man would have the fast moving clouds delayed
To celebrate he'd never be dismayed
Though his dirty laundry in the public
He washes clean to polish the frolic
Who wiggles and tickles his way beneath
The skin with ease and would leave man with death
He plays master of without foreknowledge
By so-doing he does push to the edge
None but the corpse he projects to the peak
Oblivious man's lumpy lobes has a leak
To let fluids that would flush him down the drain
And come the time he'd experience the chain
Rousseau draws attention to tell the world
Man sets his own trap for the netherworld.

Infringement

To this world we're born boys and girls, man and woman
And we grow up to place the wisdom of our clan
Above that which spins and entwines us full of life
We for granted take, and on each other with strife
Turn o'er the gift of Nature we'll ne'er be owner
Of and would we put up fences where our owner
Reckoned unnecessary; with dams built across streams
Which dams will overflow the vale to let out screams
That would echo beyond the mounts with the sound bites
Of a trumpet's blast that reminds Nature has rights
Confiscated by man who walls them in and hopes
He shall be the horse to escape the cowboys' ropes
As he plays the famed French game where winner loses
And winner man shall be with the heads in nooses.

The Burns that Soothe

Gentle with graceful gaits, she won't destroy
Not even the ants she steps on with coy
Placidity that would caress than kill
For she was blessed from birth with skills to still
A raging storm ignited by desire
To soothe that which man has scalded with fire
She blows a breeze that strokes and produces
Sweet tune in the discord that reduces
Our airs to grow the sharp teeth of frost bite
To which man has availed himself with spite
Thinking of nothing but his here and now
And making of the world his milking cow
My Burns would fuel my imagination
And leave me with unscathed emotion.

Our Rivers, Then and Now

How did our rivers become our poison?
In time past in this world was no reason
Not to drink from a river; up or down
Stream and be anxious our health would come down
And stab the drinker to end his solace
In pools that would human progress embrace
When did our rivers become our poison?
These days, men are quick to charge with treason
Those with their backs against human progress
To highlight the need for wholesome redress
Of modern backwardness that chants import
Which sweeps ruins of the world to the seaport
Whose depth has been by pollutant reduced;
Tell me why our rivers won't feel traduced!

Lauded Regression

Make progress your forte and rape the earth
In his name and your spring will not give birth
To your hopeful goal of power over
La belle dame sans pitié who's a drover
Shepherding winter, summer, fall and spring
To whom you'd dismiss the changes you bring;
Your best you have wrought with hot and cold air
Blown round the globe to leave all in despair.
Stand to the right and assert you are right
And the forfeit us over to our plight
The heat of which you would feel even more
When arts most fare and charge forevermore
Turning the tides on the head of progress
You laud. Yet, forget not headways regress!

Mess not with this Lady

When you scorch the earth, you don't see the rain
To come without fail to wash down the drain
The sticky mud your burns render porous
With a bag of products that's disastrous

When you deplete the river of fauna
How could you fail to note 'twas your downer?
In changing the system all by design
Nothing do you finish but to resign

And cast your lot to Lady Splendidness
Who would take all from you except your mess;
Tampering with that which she has intended
For you; not to be taken for granted.

Take me for the insane but you'd have signed
A warrant not to be to me assigned.

Simply Relentless

Ain't it a shame to talk over silent
Nature whose kindness never would relent
To bless man with little spices of life
Breathing in our waste and giving us life?
Splendidly noiseless and observant
She gives man no treatment of a servant
Though for real, at best, he's at her mercy;
She drives up or down his expectancy
And would determine good or bad harvest
When man grafts unlike crops to prove his best
And take simplicity for wretchedness
Far from Nature who is all usefulness
That won't want to be cheated and taken
Advantage of by him who'd not hearken.

The Wise Fool and his Land

The sagacious fool sees in the splendor
Of Nature the beauty to be ravished
And go scot-free; never to be punished.
She's poor and none would come to her succor
But her valor would rain hail on that fool
Manhandling what he's been freely given;
His reward heralded by a raven
Who'll relinquish such a fool to his school
Wherein his learning teaches him to tear
Down all with a nuclear bomb; not the spear
With which the sage of yesteryears did hunt
And today he's brandished as primitive
In a world transformed by radioactive
Waste to a land wherein man's left to grunt.

Man's Dominion

Summer just started! Why are our trees bare?
I'll not pretend not to know how unfair
Man has been to Nature which he claims his
To exploit for she is his dominion
By God given to him for a mission
He would have to accomplish without miss;
A birth right that snaps my mouth wide open
To see man like a child tear to pieces
A fly whose role is apparent without creases
In the scheme of feasting on the rotten
Having burnt out the ends of smoky days
As Eliot would have it to send roosters
Home to *Requiescat In Pace* with stars
They would they had left without any rays.

Betrayed Beloved Beauty

We shan't be the winds that bring no one good
For the bequest we shall leave our offspring
Must not have with it a taint and a string
Attached as noose for our own unborn brood
Who ask not to sojourn in a world draped
And handed down as if nothing were wrong
Though some men rape her to prove their might
Caring less how fast they rush in the night
With a tableau of fury to be sung.
Cemented leeward of the giant mountain,
The shortened of the world heave a blue cry
For a beloved betrayed beauty by dry
Scoffers all positioned right to maintain
These cries fake and far from those of the raped.

The Flags of Ghouls

We see our country change from green to brown.
Industry kills the green to build their town!
And they could care less what fate befalls us
For we are worse than the bodily pus
Festering the boils they'd bestow on the world
To get rid of those they dub primitive;
They can't accept those who are dismissive
Of the lure they flag in hope to catch fools
Who'd blow the wind that flaps the flags of ghouls
And raise the dust that doth blind from own blame
In the charge of holocaust without shame
Yet, would claim fame for the progress of change
To turn that which we know into a strange
Hideousness in the netherworld impearled.

The Gift: Land

Man's greatest gift on earth is not reason
Which can't feed man and would not take him back
When the seasons leave our spheres off the track
For physique to face the charge of treason
For he's betrayed the land on which depends
His life for rations for form and non-form
That frame both body and soul to abide
By same coin with faces none can divide
Yet, to the right are those who won't conform
And would commit treason with dynamics
Strange to reason himself who is willing
To put a wedge on warming and cooling
Dancing to a refrain akin to tricks
Pulled on the credulous who follow trends.

Motherland...

From her bosom, this land is generous
And would let man exploit her for mainstay
Yet, man seizes such occasion to stray
As he'd abuse her becoming callous
Thinking not of generations to come
He would he sculpted her to fit th'image
Of what he sees as top model on stage
Walking as would cats to say they've arrived,
Trimming themselves by being food deprived;
Which dispossession would thin skin our land
Left with only the choice of fighting back,
Which she does to show her power to crack
Down on naysayers and their cynic band
Playing their tune of deceit to bring calm...

The Alarm Bell

The heavens did not stop crying all day
And pulled the alarm bell the tornado
Was on its way to deal traffic a blow
Mile after mile on the high and freeway
Where everything came to a grinding halt
Thrown in a chaos that left none free nor high
Sending thoughts back to their very birthplace
Where man in his ramble could his greed trace
Having fed bread of sorrows to the sky
Which now in angry bouts spews back the hail
Of reckoning man will never contain;
Bearing the brunt of those who'd not refrain
And would they all gainsay to prove they're hale,
Stout, rough, and tough never will be at fault.

A Chant of Victory?

The skies flag their generosity
With a broad smile on the sun's rosy cheeks
For he'd rather not let tears flood the creeks
In which trashed world the climate is feisty
And would not take blows from man lying down
With her strength and energy from a source
Dreams will never get one to coming close
To and he'd never have an overdose
Of; and his actions would earn him remorse
Though his wish is to be unrepentant
And not to clean the world clean with clean fuel
Yet, he would his strength empty in a duel
To crush nations and retreat with a chant
Of victory and might he thinks will ne'er drown.

The Charlatan's Will

Trumped up straggly hair strands pollute the screen
Of my moral innocence in the wake
Of control charlatans willing to take
For granted our wildlife and to demean
Any who lifts his finger to defend,
Or carry a cross to protect, the land
Without mention of the erection of
An eye sore those tricksters would make their trough
And on the construction would like to stand
And blow their hot air that would have change sprouts
And throw the world into divergent camps
With rhetoric worthy of none but tramps
Ranting and *Rantering* gibberish in these bouts
Of Narcissistic folly that portend.

Talkers Talk

The tables are always round and the talks
Endless to address *see oh two* in balks
Released as they stipulate in the face
Of this task whose trace they try to erase
After injecting a dose of anger
Touching the wrong nerve of the skies who wail
And give tears free rein to rain and rain hail
To wake round table talkers from deep sleep
To take off running with no thoughts they'd creep
When, of the essence, time sings requisite
Without which nothing would be exquisite
In their world shredded for material gain
The same wraps the globe with the weakest chain
Leaving flora and fauna in danger.

No Bail

Peace making with the climate is trending
And the weather's no shoe that needs mending
To exclude the globe from catastrophe
One from which man had always dreamt he'd be
Free to see himself wiser than insight
Unveiling glacial mountain ceding way
To weathering and sending the flood his way;
By man's own doing, his land is washed down
By water whose clearness is lost to brown
And has inherited fierceness worthy
Of a hungry tiger on a healthy
Antelope in his plate waiting as meal
As would the river to seal her big deal
Swallowing all on her path with no fight.

The Scam of Man's Dominion

The sun would post its broad face smile with teeth
Gilded and glittering to reflect his joy;
Just as man would start to play with the boy
Who'd then let his frown take man to the heath
Whereto man thought he'd buried the sun's smile
And man is free, free to toy with his hand-
Made trinkets and not that which brings forth life
And would spare him the troubled life of strife
Founded upon belief in charms which stand
Not the test of time nor the change by sun
Whose ageless age will and must deal a blow
To man whose rationale grounds he can go
To any length in his pursuit of fun
For his domination is crowned by wile.

The Boat Ride

Once, a boat ride on a flooded river
I took and her waves gave me goose pimples.
The face of this flood knight stamped with dimples,
Whose beauty almost turned me a diver,
Sparked a quest as to why such adventures
I had embraced with knowledge that hungry
Hunter with no fish could make me her feed
And at worst would manure make for the reed
Within the bed on which man fed angry
Fruitless trees whose leaves evaporated
Their dew to provoke this torrential rain
That trails human endeavors in her train
And take them downstream in so elated
A state to erase traces of strictures.

The Produce of Man's Sweat

Man's shells have just pierced the heart of the earth
And have raised dust that for centuries hardened;
They rise and stroke the butts of a saddened
Sky in a cloak full with blossoms of dearth
To feed mankind the produce of his sweat
And sweat he does to prove his dominion
Over that which until death does him part
Would keep his endeavors far from their start
For he's learned all save having communion
He sees not as a being with life full
And emotions to express mistreatment
Whose rewards are in form of estrangement
From such divine sky taken for a fool
Though she is kind and not man's greatest threat.

The Rover and the River

The one on his journey to the unknown
Sees himself strong for he is made of bone
And the other on her endless journey
Knows her fluidic way to the furious sea
Whom she refuses to starve and deprive
Of her free flowing fluid tainted by man
Who sees hers as inexhaustible source
To be prodigal with using crude force
Forgetting her the font of his lifespan
And true, to a journey of no return
Both Rover and River are betrothed
But the other might end his in an urn,
Unsure to be Grecian, for full throated
Dirges to discard rivers' strife for life.

Plastics for Meals

The fish and the turtle did not invent
The plastic man serves them in the comfort
Of their dwelling place as meal for the sport
In which they shout out loud they're innocent
As such man's guilt is without a question
Throwing scraps left and right and front and back
In a frenzy of one who's taken crack
And with turmoil of atmospheric heat
And cold challenging him into a feat
Wherein he lands on a distinctive space
And receives a garnished platter of woes
That blinds him to the effect of his race
To amass junk that leaves him in the throes
Of twisters that come with writ of sanction.

Far from Man's Call

Hunting and gathering? Man's life ought to be
And for sustenance! Not to feed callous
Greed that changes scavengers to monstrous
Creatures who won't, like bees, produce honey
But would think they could outdrink the ocean
Or outshine the Sun and evaporate
Every droplet of water therein held
In hope their fate is not to the sea weld
Which shall come to pass to say who is great:
Greedy Man or generous Mother Earth?
Thoughtless Man ceaselessly taps from her womb
Which yields black and white gold then man makes bomb
To fight for who keeps all and who's in dearth;
And the victor wins standing ovation.

The Arbiter

When man plays foul, Nature raises her flag
For eyes that can see and if not blasts sounds
For ears that can hear; and if not burns grounds
For farms to grow no vine that makes man brag.
Nature makes man her horse whose rein she pulls
To drop into him a jolt of current
Just enough to wake man to his conceit
In which his life is marked by self-deceit
And hopes to take refuge in a convent
At the end of his pervasive foul play
When he becomes wizened and feels the heat
He'd been giving the world in his mad feat
One he could stop but would he seized the day
And took all who play by the rules for fools.

Man's Rap Sheet

Man curls his foolishness from a cheat sheet
Without knowing the sun, moon, and stars keep
And track his delinquencies without sleep;
With all minutiae drawn on a rap sheet.
Yet, man sees himself brainy without
And questions not wherefrom comes his brilliance
To treat the planet with such disrespect
That would leave a mindful mouth circumspect
Of statements that are garbed in defiance,
Beautifully colored winged butterfly
Mummified for exhibit in a case
Vitrified by toppling the moon's phase
And warming the globe with over supply
Of chest thumping thoughtlessness man is stout.

The Sun's Tears

Looking at the Sun frown to let his tears
Flow and drum the roof tops and lull to sleep
Give reasons not to stay up and count sheep
Then collapse in the sheepish trap of fears
Brought about by a smear on the sun's face
Left here by mindless humans' disconnect
From the reality of a sober globe
Garbed in a low profile who needs no probe
But humans leading a picture-perfect
Life which our parents of yesteryears lived,
Preserving nature for posterity
Treating their surroundings with dignity
For such was as is the way we'd survived.
Now? Won't we make the sun smile in our space?

Reality Comes Home

The glowing ambers of this universe
Comes in response to man's brutal treatment
Of the globe who'd been ravished and misspent
For gains that won't be able to reverse
The havoc inflicted on the environs
Upon which is entrenched mortal's life force
For man's arrogance to delight with spite
And ride this willing horse without respite;
Holding all in nature will take their course.
And their course they take and man to the grave
Wherein in his wildest of dreams he'd not
Projected this occurrence would be wrought
And worse to him who sees himself so brave
To beat in the quagmire marshland herons.

The Childishness of Science

Man's oppression to the environment
Crowns the limits of man's foolish wisdom
To claim inheritance of a kingdom
In a desert where stood a monument
Of desire to make the highest mountain
From the garbage of human emptiness
That peoples and clouds souls in their judgment
To pick and choose between hideous government
Wheeling to style climate change brazenness
And the deal of learning noticing rise
And fall, without stew, in temperatures
Cutting across the globe and its creatures
Paying, with their lives as martyrs, the price
For a universe man cannot sustain.

How Come Our Seasons...

The quest: "in thunder, lightning, or in rain?"
Bespeak of all whose firm embrace darkness
Craves never to leave as their cleverness
Gets them deeper and deeper down the drain
In which heat, moisture, and discomfort rule
Ruling those clever men who leap before
They look at the sore their lore has in store
For them and which their thoughts held was of yore
And had them delight with joy we deplore.
The seasons go before they even come
Yet, clever men hold fast to merriment
And dream of it and nothing else to come
Sweep away this chimeric development
They use to trash people with at their school.

Deluded Development

What a delicacy to taste the sky
Blue show butter melting skills in water,
One which has repudiated waste matter
And man whose real love is to see her cry
For him to grin and flash his teeth for smile!
That glaze and glow follow the delusion
Of anticipated development
Which is well packaged windstorm some government
Foments, sows, and grows out of proportion
Taking fauna and flora defending
Champions for buffoons retailing antics
Not worth wasting time to crush them with tricks
Expressly when abusage is trending;
And looking after the earth? Out of style!

The Blame

When foul, the weather's always at fault
With a mountain of blames heaped by man, blind
To his belligerence on this kind find
He's always claimed to be his by default
And with astute stubbornness and disdain
He rapes and would refuse to reap the grapes
Of wrath the weather has favored to grow
Without care man claims her change is too slow
Her course uncertain with no chance she drapes
The face of the globe with a knockout bout
One day were one to track the route of myths
That her coming would leave a trail of filth
Too difficult to make a roundabout
Turn before the fury man saw was gain.

The Summons We Serve

The weather only sneezed and we're walled in
With our backs turned against the same summons
We'd served her in hopes we'd send our demons
Out after making sure our gains stayed in.
We castoff thoughts of what will be in store
Were she to cough out her bilious cyclone
Which she sometimes does with the head-strong firm
On their stance that she'd never make them squirm;
For better than her they'll sit on a throne
Covered with gold and by their own hands made
For none but themselves and in their weird world
In which they refuse to see they have culled
Everything synergetic to be paid
Yet, Ms. Weather's slap will settle the score.

Let the Sky Rise...

Man may spend time sky-rising his cities,
His love and passion for development
In whose name he spites our environment
On whom life depends for her sweet pasties
Served to gluttonous man whose voracious,
Wet appetite, and ocean deep stomach
Would never have enough fish to fill it
For good old greed elevates his spirit.
Man with snout, claws, and feet of an aardvark
Becomes not the earth pig but one buried
In his junkyard of accumulated
Scrap metal with which he won't be parted;
But would crave favor from him be curried
And not from him with a mind that's curious.

Truck Load of Joy

The pine trees whispered the gentle breeze
That caressed ears and lulled babies to sleep
Sound and never know what it means to weep
And to stay beaming with joy without crease.
Now man's rid his view of the trees he takes
To be the prod of his regressive state
And so is the music gone with the wind
That claims to be of change that leaves man blind
To the naked plants on which hangs his fate.
When the weather comes to pay man's handwork,
He'll exhibit the noose around his neck
And call it improvement he gives a peck
To; then pretend his joy would fill a truck
Just to garner his dreams trapped in earthquakes.

Crops from the Playgrounds

These peaks, hills, slopes and valleys are playgrounds
Whereon man takes a chance and digs own grave
Turning them inside-out to show he's brave
And the grounds the game that would not need hounds
To be hunted, caught, and feasted upon.
Life's devoid of accidents and chances.
Man's wish to fall trees, divert waterways,
Heat the globe, are chessmen with which man plays;
Cheering he'd win over these grievances
He'd like to clear himself of and be free
And free he'll be free when he comes to terms
With the globe's need for care not his firms
That pollute and let man go on a spree
With yields from global destruction for fun.

Making of the Fire

Our fights have been for a place in the sun
Taking no credit we'd been making fire
That would burn us to ash swept down the mire
Without a need to trigger a cannon
Or fight a war with guns and bathe the land
With the blood of innocence as would man
When he hides in the clouds above the skies
Of other lands playing the game of spies
Willing to execute their wicked plan,
Blind to the clouds' desire to regulate
The sun's blades' sharpness in slashing the earth
And gaping open wombs to risks of dearth
As barrenness would rush in and not wait
For reigns that would never hug the land.

Warming Doubts

These sailing clouds are not lost ships at sea
They are simply running away from waste
Man throws into space in his racy haste
To stretch his tentacles above the tree
In his quest for Eden and the senses
To embrace that with which he is endowed:
"Skinny, tiny and far from sufficient
For that almighty giant man, a sentient
Homo sapiens", who in defiance has vowed
To rid the skies of any sun screen clouds
For 'tis his right and place to call the shots
And pop the cyclones with clicks of snapshots
That would dispel him myths of warming doubts
His reckless efforts ground his plight's basis.

Victors vs Ms. Weather Loser

Belligerent interventions pay off
And bring in their train a payload of yields
Harvested in the ruins of battlefields
Where victors kill for loots that they so love
More than the ecosphere, they'd not protect.
So must man aggress the environment
And garner the same in the aftermath
For in man's calculations, all is math
At work to evaluate development.
Ms. Weather Loser would have the last word
And surely the last laugh which is the best
For at last, man's lust would be laid to rest
With the sword entombed to avoid discord
Then man would treat Ms. Loser with respect.

Discovery at Four

When rain came it meant playtime for children;
As one, I had figured it out myself
Thinking the rain will always be itself
Coming when it wanted for the children;
We pampered the cat and mouse game we played
Running around, in the rain, half-naked.
For me, it was the source of life to be
Savored and not let it hide like a flea
As it sips tea when man becomes wicked
And cheats on and steals from rain the color
Of life it comes and paints for eyes
To feast on and never know woes and cries.
The ball man must play to avoid dolor
Not the hasty quirk he has thus displayed.

Shackles of Accumulation

Man falters. The rains decorate the sky
With her commanding black robe and her grey
Hair is hardly seen for she won't display
It to fool man he has had a good try!
When blackened, the skies fall in an irate
Feat; their tears overflow for man to pay
For breaking the law like a bird of prey
Poaching and feasting when he's not hungry
While the poor and hungry crave to be free
From the shackles of accumulation
Fastened by the greedy open ended
Hungry grotto that cannot be tended
To because her grip on air pollution,
Cannot but the skies' tears exacerbate.

The Sound of Judgment

The skies are clad in their robe of a judge
And carry the gavel behind an oak
Table from which responses they would poke
Out of man who has smeared them and would dodge
When on the table gavel drums the sound
Of judgment for crimes, passive or active
Man has all along thought to get away
With just to discover there is no way
Out of the lethal waste he's piled to give
The illusion of his innovation
And development projecting chimneys
That vomit soot to give the skies the keys
Into the courtroom where reprobation
Is washed, trounced, and left on a quaky ground.

She's here to Judge

To judge the earth she comes with equity
To jostle man's brain in the direction
Of his crime of commodification
Of the globe's generous gift of plenty
To a world wherein man's folly runs wild;
Burn fossil fuel for feasts around his tomb
Unbeknownst the judge brings retribution
For unruliness, dumping without caution
And painting the climate as a coxcomb.
Mother Nature has invisible hands
And would flag her red card to stop careless
Man from treating her as a meaningless
Constituent, of this life, that understands
Not flies suffer in the hands of a child.

The Trespassers

The heavens are not the work of man's hands
Yet, man would devour them like hungry hounds
And take them for trespassers on the grounds
The heavens are but a toy in his hands;
He ignores vengeance is a dish served cold
And eaten with chopsticks of deep regrets
Prepared by him who rubbishes patience
And flags gold dust, the price for indulgence
To absolve man of self-inflicted threats
Now come to hunt and haunt their own creator
And in this game the player is made game
To be shamed after his vain brawls for fame;
Man is thus carved out as the impostor
Far from him who considered himself bold.

First Day of Spring 2016

This day defies the nature of winter
And leaves the heavens with an open tear
Gland; tearing not rain but snow that brings fear,
Leaves one in the grip of Harold Pinter
Whose world is ensnared by such a spirit
Awondering the becoming of a bride
Clad in white the day her fresh should sheen green
And tickle the emotion of the keen
Who need bury their indifference and pride.
But alas! This day drags in all else but
The luster of the sun on leaves dancing;
The flora abandoned to frost biting
Hard and leaving the city's streets all shut
As spring walks in timidly and discrete.

The Bride and Her Groom

Baltimore the bride awaits a rebirth
While the groom is given a cold hand shake
That he cannot reject from the snow flake
Who shows up to conjure nothing but death;
This greedy groom has turned his bride inside-
Out, for the richness of her womb turns sane
Minds to lose their rationale and aspire
After the absurd sense of the empire
Leading man to glory that is all vain
In which vanity is celebrated
Material possession accrued without
Forethought one should for the spiritual scout
For the crux of life to be arrested
And locked in while warring is put outside.

Making the Weather New

Lust for industry transports man in greed
To the heights of unstoppable desire
Blind to his predicament in a mire
Where life would mark an end for his strange breed.
Man's industrial machines in their rage spew
Smoke and smog that poison and choke rain clouds
Who embrace not those with other plumage
Whitened not by burns yet, colored by age
In her grey wisdom pushing away crowds
And falling leaves off the trees as she crawls
Through the haze she uses to faze the sun
From striking the ball that grows his home fun
By letting concrete walls stage city brawls
Through what man conceives he'd turn weather new

Drill and Frack

Drill and drill; frack and frack! You'd make money
You'd pass for light and then bear the brunt
As drill and frack will have you make a grunt
Under such weight laden by a looney.
Thirst and thirst after greenbacks; you would know
Not the joy a loving mother would plant
With hopes children's garden grows wood-sorrel
Around which offspring hop like a squirrel
In delight with gathered nuts without want.
You may want to drill again for the gain
You'd love8 to dream accrues from your reckless
Treatment of treasures not for your thoughtless
Operations stowed and which with disdain
You pump out of the well as means to grow.

Robes of Hopes

Time has laid its foundation and upon
It, has, with care, strata after strata
Built a structure which man needs not scatter
With the brain of a sheep life will go on
And on with him spared his greed flagged misdeed
Bent on unearthing the juice in which float
This bubble wherein Man's wedded to dream
Of making his locale *better* with steam
As nothing but steam engine moves a boat.
Man's is architectural intention
To move the world with cloud slowing speed bumps
Without regard the masses dwell in slumps
Which have been erected by corruption
Whose colorful robes raise hopes they'd be freed.

The Clement Avenger

Man's folly sparks heavens wrath and anger.
This foolishness man styles development;
Crime against Mother-Nature, the clement
Who'd been pushed to become an avenger
Showing man's robe unfit for any creed
With claims of a gift that postures him right.
Right man claims and claims that which is not his,
Including that to make snakes laugh, not hiss
As they see birds drop dead and not their bright
Plumages upon which these crawlies could
Not smile their way to moving their bowels
As man does smile his way to drilling wells
With belief the world, he has understood
Should move fast without heed haste is less speed.

Of Man's Forte

In her rotation and revolution
The earth has never been in such haste
For he steals away both savor and taste
And leaves nothing behind but revulsion
And such a lesson man has not taken
Seriously claiming reason his forte
And would with it turn the world upside-down
And have all those who oppose him put down
For daring to bar man from his mainstay,
The muddy black gold drilled to burn the world
To extinction in the name of progress
That leaves man with no choice of a redress;
Even though from outside it is impearled.
The earth's movement must be, by man, hearken.

The Lessons We Refuse to Learn

They did not make their way here as rumors
We saw the hurricanes, the tsunamis,
The wildfire, the volcanoes, and the freeze
Not forgetting the heat and the horrors
They planted in our minds we toss aside
For the chimera we design upstairs
To steal the show from a nodding lizard
That we can brave and survive a blizzard
That could have turned our lives into nightmares
Yet, we quest not whence and where they come from
For being the culprit behind the show
Man has nurtured without waiting this blow
Who storms her way in the like of a prom
Queen who would push all other girls aside.

G.M. Splendor

We love to death to beautify this land
With genetically modified trees
And believe this prettification frees
Us from the pollen that's our sinking sand
Yet the tropics greet twisters blowing dust
The masses would take for their snuff and sniff
And, still have to survive the particles
Which will push them to ponder manacles
That have steered us to the edge of this cliff
Where we are left struggling not to fall off
Having inhaled a good dose of pollens
That tracked and dragged us out of our kitchens
Where thoughts jumped out to be shielded from cough
And lust only after that splendid crust.

To Twirl the Truth?

We nod to ourselves and would want to glow
Then plop like dead birds not their plumages
Yet, fail to see wisdom in these pages
Who to us speak and so does their echo
Drum in our eardrums the care we need give
The environment within which we dwell
And pretend, over her, we have dominion
When we can't protect this gorgeous minion
But would go a long way to swell and twirl
The truth with our mastery as true agents
Contesting same reason we claim to be
Our God-given sweet and tasty honey:
"Around which science builds walls like regents
Barring princes from thrones for which they live."

Pool of Nightmares

Were the earth greedy man, she would have drunk
And stored everything liquid that exists
Like mongering man who quaffs and can't desist:
From the portentous sign showing he'd flunk
In his vain moves to keep his powder dry
Without care for the fate he presses to stalk
Calm and quiet Mother Nature who fights
Not back not because she feels not her plights
But because she'd not take on a bulwark
Man has made of cards and, like a child, dreams
His fortification invincible;
Which fortune to her is reversible
To leave man bathing in nightmares and screams
With him wishing he could live to comply.

The Rainmaker

We greet their illusion of rain making
Not without thoughts such rain is devil's piss
From his fire lake as we give him a hiss;
For, lauding him would be our unmaking
And we cannot afford to be ensnared
As such torrent is but a preamble
To a synthetic drought in those pipelines
Whose detonation would tone down landmines
When the world has lost all in a gamble
Who sweet-talked his way to those with their brain
To the right warming up to inaction
And claiming global warming pure fiction
At works to stall all what they'd have to gain;
If the light of their burnt fossil fuel flared.

The Habit of Perdition

By day, man skillfully transforms the earth
Into the waiting room, the waiting room
Of hell which to clean he won't have a broom
To sweep away the damages and dearth
Brought daily by toxic smoke from chimneys
That besmirch the blue of the skies with soot
To leave poor little me in the muddle
For Blake to have my fingers make sparkle
Those chimneys that man did clog with the loot
Evaporating as man turns the earth
Inside out for the content of her womb
For which he would chest thump for the coxcomb
Who hails man at the origin of his birth
Knowing not he brings himself to his knees.

Where the Change Hides

To map this territory, the thunder roars
To remind man of the reckless treatment
He visits upon the environment
And hopes that he and no one but he soars
To self-envision the golden eagle
With command baton to prey on the South
Where in the years of yore men were carted
As chattels destined to be marketed
Where warming and cooling hide in their mouth
Wherein birthing capital thrives without
Care for the protection of the layer
Of ozone depleted by that player
Only interested in fly-fishing trout;
His sure way to avoid feeding beagle.

Cat on the Right

To be on the right does not make one right
Not even when with a trumpet he blasts
His wisdom in not turning out the last
As those left on the left shoulder this plight
And weather the storm directed their way
While keeping the finger pointing at them
As the agential culprits who rain down
Blizzards, Sunrays, and hail that wear a frown
And would never hesitate to condemn
Those who to hide their ignorance espouse
Non-familiarity with the science
Of the hills and forests they, like giants,
Crush as would a cat an ungrateful mouse
Yet all we have is the grace of our stay.

The Kitten and the Mirror

With such over-processed hair on his back
That kitten perceives himself a tiger
After gulping six glasses of lager
And looking into a glass with a crack
Showing him a skyline as the way home
And this route, he takes blind to the rising
And falling temperatures that he styles
A vague echo from many million miles
Coming to steal a show from a rising
Star who with the snap of the fingers can
Resolve the world's problem with a command
To fix his country without reprimand
For in the jungle big cats reign not man
Whose presence would send a pussy to roam.

Weather Report

Rains all afternoon with overcast sky
Is the weatherman's holler to conceal
The culprit who, to show off, dines on veal
And would whine and wine without being shy
Our fingers are pointing at his mansion
Wherein the fossilized animal bones
Keep the glow in the hearth of his heartless
House wherefrom smoke escapes to create the mess
In which he traps us with the skill he hones
To unveil in it we're the lawbreakers
Because, as he claims, the hot air we blow
In union with the disdain we for him grow
Make us offenders not the icebreakers
That give him license to split his ration.

The Watch Word

The clouds from their throne up above climb down
To earth without hope to find peace for sure
As they sail through sustaining this fissure
Provoked by the crime with which man would crown
His sorrows and claim industry his strength;
One that exudes his scarecrow shabbiness
To reflect the aftermath of the storm
Passing to bring home this new word: reform
With which word man won't he had a business
For trade entails depletion of resources
To maximize profitability
Which to man is the only reality
He protects to overwork these horses
Orwell had christened Boxer for their strength

Our Roads: The Elect

We have never ceased to stomp on our roads
Who have now been reduced to riverbeds
And we quest not the criminal who shreds
The environment and provokes these loads
Of rains that elect our streets as the ring
Within which they dish out this knock-out bout
And press those of us left on the margins
Never to have these big dreams about gins
Turned rivers in which we see rainbow trout
Swim their arrogant way to dominance;
A mirror image of those at the helm
Who, in our portrayal, see the problem
They would neither solve nor take cognizance
Of; this strain by the rain our reigning king.

Of Seasons and Reasons

The season we met did not give me a reason
But after many came and went, reasons abound
With me hanged in and unable to touch the ground
My senses point to, far down in the abysm;
Your departure digs deep and bleeds this hurting heart
Dying you stayed on to grace it with happiness
Yet, wisdom tells the dearest know when to say quit
And as I listen, I crave I got my ears fit
To drink the story of a parting, in sadness,
Drape like the rain clouds who come to veil the sun
In their marriage with ignorance they're just passing
And won't catch a glimpse of the ghost with a passing
Glance as they desire to hijack the show for fun
Unlike the ancients who were serious the world's flat.

For Growth & Profit

Let every second be a new second
Let every minute be a new minute
And let not the hour jot down the minute
Let reasons come first and seasons second
For time as man has always come and gone
Without taking to its resting abode
The magnificence that adorns the face
Of the universe, an unchanging place
To climate change sceptics who think a goad
Falls on their backs and without rational,
From fanatics who sleep, breathe, eat, and drink
The scare they serve to those who do not think
For if they do, they would see national
Growth and profit shielded by a cannon.

Lay not to Rest

I thought I would lay this volume to rest
With my eyes on growth and profit alone
Not the cannon which blinds eyes with a stone,
Having failed to do that which it does best;
Kill, spill, and waste the blood of innocence
Regardless of whether the weather heats
Up or cools down far from the bottom line
Which quest for the silver in the skyline
To make a case with the help of pink sheets
Whose answers to the fauna and flora
Are all wrong and lead the environment
Under water where the Monarch, Torment
Reigns absolute with baits of chimera
Brandished to man as his life's quintessence.

Flooding the Bushes

My glands open to pour out their content
Of lachrymal fluids for doubters to laugh
As they think me foolish crying for love,
Of the art most fair they joy to torment
In the throes of sadomasochism
To stroke a smirk and a smile on their face
That will see hills, mountains, and valleys run
Down as they call the shots they name big gun
Which blasts its toxic smoke into the space
Thus opening the floodgates of tears from eyes
Whose sharpness defies those of hunting spears
And whose voice sing to move like Burning Spear's
That warms the heart and not melting ice
On which tormentors build their bushism.

Their Spill, My Tears

Their spill flooded our coast as did my tears
Their arrogance on which they do stand tall
With ignorance pride comes before a fall
They view as a commodity so scarce
Not as my body transformed into one
So common that 'tis just a bottom line
That the best of my kind is dismembered,
Burnt, and buried not to be remembered
For they are the clouds that won't let sun shine
To brighten our industry burning out
The green that pollute our beautiful sight
And leaves us nowhere else but in a tight
Corner with neither choice nor a way out
But to leave the world in quest of a fan.